Tugs

in Colour-U.K.

Introduction

The first two years of the new millennium saw profound changes in the ownership of tug fleets in the UK. The Howard Smith group, an Australian company which had taken over Alexandra Towing in 1994, was itself taken over by another Australian company, Adsteam Marine Ltd. The latter company then claimed ownership of the largest tug fleet in the world. Early in 2000, Cory Towage was taken over by Wijsmuller and the tugs were painted in the new company's colours. The paint barely had time to dry before it was announced that Wijsmuller had been taken over by Svitzer, a Danish company which is part of the A P Møller group. Again the tugs were repainted. This album reflects these changes and provides an opportunity to see new tugs, old tugs in new liveries, and old tugs in old liveries!

One of the virtues of large conglomerates is that the resources can be transferred so it is becoming increasingly common to see Adsteam and Svitzer tugs being redeployed between various locations. Indeed, Adsteam has brought tugs from Australia to the Thames but, at the time of writing, there is no sign of Svitzer transferring tugs between its traditional base in Scandinavia and the UK. It is interesting to observe that Adsteam announced "a comprehensive review of the company's operations" in mid-2003 as this book is being compiled.

In all books such as this, it is difficult to know what to include and, conversely, what to omit. Some preserved tugs are included but the vast majority of tugs featured are shiphandling vessels. Tugs used for civil engineering work do not feature prominently. It is equally difficult to know how much technical information to include. Reference is made to the varying types of propulsion units but no attempt is made to explain these. Readers requiring further information should look elsewhere for this information. Figures have been given for the engine power and bollard pull for as many tugs as possible. However, no guarantee is given that these figures are correct. Different sources give different figures, especially for bollard pull.

Acknowledgements

My requests for photographs of specific tugs or specific areas were met with an enthusiastic response and I have been faced with an embarrassment of riches. There is enough excellent material to produce a follow-up volume if readers decide it would be welcome. There will certainly be a similar book about tugs elsewhere in Europe to follow this one. Grateful thanks to those individuals who have loaned me their precious colour transparencies - specific acknowledgement accompanies each photograph. A general acknowledgement is offered here to the port companies who have permitted photography on their estate.

I must also record my thanks to those who have responded so well to requests for information, notably Chris Jones. Much of the information about the tugs has been built up over the years from tug crews, and from the writings of Jack Gaston who has been an acknowledged expert on the UK tug scene for many years. Written sources used include *Lloyd's Register of Shipping*, *Sea Breezes*, *Marine News*, *Cory Towage* (by W J Harvey), *Blow Five* (by W B Hallam), *United Towing 1920 - 1990* (by Alan Ford) and *Seahorses of the Tees* (by John Proud). Once again, Gil Mayes has checked through draft pages of the book, corrected many errors, and added to the information about the vessels. Errors that remain are my own responsibility.

Finally, I wish to acknowledge the work of Amadeus Press in bringing the book to what I hope readers will consider to be a suitable conclusion. At a time when conventional print media seem to be under attack from digital material, it remains my firm conviction that it is impossible to surpass the content of a well-produced book.

Bernard McCall
Portishead, February 2004

Front cover : A colourful view of Alexandra Towing tugs at Swansea in May 1988.

Back cover : The **Point Gilbert**'s name does not reflect any earlier fleet nomenclature and the reason for this is that she was built to serve the Come-by-Chance oil refinery in Canada. She is powered by a Ruston-Paxman engine of 2640bhp. Built by Richard Dunston, Hessle, and launched on 14 April 1972, she and sistership **Point James** returned to the UK in 1979 and Cory Towage relocated them to Avonmouth, the **Point Gilbert** arriving during June 1980. The **Point Gilbert** was able to outlive her sistership in the Bristol Channel because she was modified in 1986 by the fitting of a powerful retractable azimuthing bow thruster. This increased her bollard pull to 45 tonnes. A further modification was the addition of a towing winch on the aft deck and towing hook on the forecastle. These modifications enabled her to work effectively as stern tug for the large vessels using the Royal Portbury Dock.
(Both photographs by Bernard McCall)

The **Lowgarth** was one of several similar tugs built in the mid-1960s for R & J H Rea Ltd at the Lowestoft yard of Richards (Shipbuilders) Ltd. By the mid-1970s, this fleet had come within the control of Cory Ship Towage Ltd which was itself a division of Ocean Transport & Trading Ltd. The **Lowgarth** was launched on 21 December 1964. She has a Ruston & Hornsby engine of 920bhp driving a single screw rotating in a steerable Kort nozzle, giving her a bollard pull of 15 tonnes. She spent her working life on the Bristol Channel, usually in the South Wales ports. In the spring of 1997, she was laid up awaiting sale in Bristol's City Docks as seen here and was then reported to have been sold for use on the River Weaver but she was thought to be too deep draughted for use on this river and nearby Weaver Navigation. Early in 2003, she was observed in Ipswich with no definite news of her intended use.

(Bernard McCall)

The **John King** has certainly had a chequered career. This was her original name when built in Bristol in 1936 for C J King & Sons Ltd. In 1970, she was sold to another Bristol company, F A Ashmead & Sons, by whom she was renamed **Peter Leigh**. In 1978, she was renamed **Pride** and then took the name **Durdham** in 1986. She found herself in difficulties off the South Devon coast after an engine breakdown on 31 October 1988 and had to be escorted into Salcombe by the local lifeboat. She was repaired and returned to the Bristol Channel. At the time, it was reported that she was being used to collect appropriate vessels for a new Coastal Forces museum being established in Gloucester. By the mid-1990s, she had come into the care of the Bristol Industrial Museum and was restored to full working order under her original name. In the summer of 2002, she found herself back in use in rather surprising circumstances when she was used for several days to assist the coaster **Lucie** in the City Docks as part of a play written to recall the work of local dockers in the 1950s. Her presence certainly added to the authenticity of the performances.

(Bernard McCall)

The **Mayflower** has the distinction of being the oldest tug in Britain and her survival is remarkable. She was built in 1861 by Stothert & Marten at Hotwells in Bristol for the Gloucester & Berkeley Canal Company. Intended for work on the canal linking Sharpness to Gloucester, she also found work in the Bristol Channel as far as Portishead. In 1876, she was fitted with a new boiler and condenser, and then in 1899 she was fitted with yet another new boiler along with a new compound condensing engine, funnel and propeller. Apart from the boiler which was replaced in 1909, this machinery remains. In 1948, she passed into the ownership of the newly-formed British Waterways who decided against equipping her with a diesel engine. Her steam machinery was very useful in the harsh winter of 1962/63 when the engines of the diesel tugs could not be started and she was used along with the **Primrose** (see page 30). She was laid up in 1964 and sold for scrap three years later. Even had she been demolished then, she would have seen over a century of work. She was not scrapped, but survived vandalism and a sinking to be purchased by the City of Bristol Museum in 1981. She has been fully restored and offers trips around the dock area and into the Bristol Channel where she was photographed on 12 September 1997.

(Danny Lynch)

The **Speedwell** was also constructed for use on the Gloucester - Sharpness Canal, and has the distinction of being the last conventional tug to be purpose-built for this use. She was built at the Thorne yard of Richard Dunston Ltd and arrived at Sharpness from the builders on 29 February 1968. Of 330bhp, she was intended for use in shiphandling but as the number of seagoing ships visiting Gloucester declined and many ships calling at Sharpness are now equipped with bow thrusters, she is now rarely used for her original purpose but handles barges being used for various engineering projects along the canal. The current livery of the tug is hardly pleasing! She is seen at Sharpness of 13 February 2002.

(Dominic McCall)

Appropriately, the **Avongarth** is seen in the River Avon on 25 February 2000 when she was assisting the Russian coaster **Leonid Leonov**, a rare arrival in Bristol's City Docks. The **Avongarth** represents a design of vessel which has become familiar in many north European ports, the tugs having been imported from Japan. Launched at Kobe on 19 April 1980 and completed two months later, she was built as **Iwashima Maru**. Her two Niigata engines, with a total of 2600bhp, drive twin Z-Peller propulsion units giving a bollard pull of 35 tonnes. Unusually, she was delivered from Japan as deck cargo on the heavy-lift ship **Project Arabia** along with a slightly larger tug destined for the J P Knight fleet on the Medway. The tug was towed to Avonmouth by the **Point Gilbert** and, after being refitted in dock and at Sharpness, entered service as **Avongarth**.

(Bernard McCall)

The last decade has seen several important takeovers in the UK towage industry. One of the most significant was that of Cory Towage Ltd by the Dutch Wijsmuller company in January 2000. Within 18 months, this company had itself been taken over by the Danish Svitzer group. A consequence of these changes is that the tugs involved appeared in a succession of liveries. These three views of the 1995-built **Portgarth** illustrate the three liveries of some former Cory tugs. The **Portgarth** is one of several vessels in this book to have been built by the Damen Group in Holland as one of a standard type, in her case a Damen ASD 3110 tug. Indeed she has the distinction of being the first shiphandling tug to be delivered to British owners by the Damen group. She was launched at Damen's Gorinchem yard on 23 February 1995 and entered service on the Bristol Channel in spring 1995, having left the builder's yard on 31 March that year. A powerful tug, she is equipped with two Stork Wartsila 9F 240 main engines of 4050bhp in total and twin Aquamaster 1701 propulsion units. These are multi-directional propellers mounted at the stern and provide a bollard pull of 50 tonnes.

Above left, the **Portgarth** wears her original Cory colours, whilst in the above view she wears Wijsmuller colours. Her present Svitzer livery is seen on the left.

(All photographs by Bernard McCall)

Launched at the Great Yarmouth yard of Richards (Shipbuilders) Ltd on 17 July 1980, the **Sea Endeavour** had a surprisingly conventional appearance and equally conventional propulsion system. At a time when various systems were being introduced, she had a single Ruston engine of 3150bhp driving a single fixed-pitch propeller rotating in a steerable Kort nozzle. On trials, she achieved a bollard pull of 46.5 tonnes - an impressive figure for a tug of this design. She entered service at Avonmouth in the fleet of C J King & Sons Ltd, making a six-strong fleet. On 1 February 1983, the King tug fleet merged with that of Cory Ship Towage Ltd to become Cory-King Towage. Only two King tugs survived the merger, the **Sea Endeavour** and

Sea Challenge. She has had five different liveries whilst based at the same port. As the Port of Bristol byelaws at the time prescribed a minimum of two towage companies in the port, Cory Towage chartered the two tugs from Cory-King. Initially she wore C J King colours and then had both variations of Cory colours. Here she is seen in the colourful Wijsmuller livery but was then repainted in Svitzer colours. The arrival of the **Svitzer Bristol** in the Bristol Channel in mid-2003 (see page 9) resulted in her transfer to the Swansea fleet.

(Dominic McCall)

The **Svitzer Bristol** arrived at her new home port on 15 July 2003. Following the many changes mentioned on page 2, the Svitzer group had come to own 240 tugs in 24 countries at the time of this book's publication. This vessel is the first of four ordered from Spanish shipbuilder Astilleros Zamakona, of Viscaya. She was followed in late September by the **Svitzer Brunel**, and two similar tugs were destined for delivery to the Mersey. The choice of names has certainly raised eyebrows for it signals the end of a long tradition of perpetuating names associated with the tug fleets in those areas of the UK where Svitzer now owns the fleets. The **Svitzer Bristol** is a tractor tug with two Niigata main engines of 4087bhp driving a pair of Niigata azimuthing propulsion units. A bollard pull of 58.5 tonnes was achieved on trials. The tug has a firefighting capability, the monitors being supplied via the prominent red-painted main. The photograph depicts her leaving Avonmouth on 22 August 2003.

(Bernard McCall)

The **Cultra**, photographed at Newport on 6 February 1983, bears a name not normally associated with South Wales tugs. A single screw vessel of 1260bhp, she was launched on 8 March 1962 at the T Mitchison yard on the River Tyne at Gateshead for Belfast owner John Cooper Ltd whose fleet was taken over by R & J H Rea Ltd in 1969, this company becoming Cory Ship Towage in the following year. She was transferred to Newport in late 1980 and was displaced from there by the arrival of the former Ems tug **Norderney** in 1983 (see page 12). At this point, she was sold to Frank Pearce (Tugs) Ltd, of Poole, by whom she was renamed **Pullwell**. Two years later she left UK ownership and was purchased by Greek owners who renamed her **Polikos**. Her Polar engine of 1260bhp drives a single controllable pitch propeller and she has a bollard pull of 20 tonnes. Details of the **Danegarth** will be found on page 15.

(Bernard McCall)

With fewer large vessels using the ports and because of the better manoeuvrability of the remaining large ships, Svitzer Marine cut the number of tugs serving ports in south-east Wales to only three during the first half of 2003. A casualty of the cutback was the **Emsgarth**. Built at the Cassens shipyard in Emden in 1975 as **Juist** for local owners and launched on 28 January 1975, she was acquired by Cory Ship Towage Ltd in March 1984, thus following the **Norderney**. She has a Motorenwerk Mannheim engine of 2400bhp driving a single fixed-pitch propeller rotating in a steerable Kort nozzle and this gives her a bollard pull of 27 tonnes. The transporter bridge in the background identifies the location as Newport Docks as the **Emsgarth** passes through in Wijsmuller livery on 4 April 2002.

(Danny Lynch)

11

The funnel design of a black diamond on white band was the traditional one for Cory vessels, reminding onlookers of the company's historical involvement in the coal trade. Many lamented the disappearance of that traditional funnel design the mid-1980s. Here we see it to good effect on two tugs working at Cardiff. The 1972-built *Gwentgarth* was normally stationed Newport. Like the *Emsgarth* on the previous page, she was originally based at Emden, having been built at the Cassens yard in Emden in 1972. Launched on 27 October 1972, she had worked as *Norderney* at Emden and arrived at Newport on June 1983. She is powered by a single Motorenwerk Mannheim engine of 1300bhp driving a single fixed-pitch propeller rotating a steerable Kort nozzle, giving her a bollard pull of 22 tons.

The *Holmgarth* was built in 1979 by Scott & Sons, Bowling, for the Cory fleet in Cardiff along with sister vessel *Hallgarth*. Her two Ruston diesel engines of 2190bhp each drive a Voith Schneider unit and produce a bollard pull of 23.5 tonnes. They were the first Voith Schneider tugs built for a South Wales port. The *Holmgarth* was launched on 18 December 1978. In the autumn of 1992 she was transferred to the Mersey and became the first Voith Schneider tractor tug to be employed on this river. She returned to the Bristol Channel in 1998 and has remained there apart from a brief stay in Dublin during the summer of 199

The *Gwentgarth* and *Bargarth* assist a large vessel out of Cardiff in dramatic evening light on 1 November 1985. On this date Cory Ship Towage Ltd became simply Cory Towage Ltd. Associated with this was a change of livery, the "new" livery being exemplified by the two tugs. The livery was very like that worn by the tugs when they were in the ownership of R and J H Rea Ltd.

The *Gwentgarth* was sold to Spanish owners in 1997 and left Newport on 30 June 1997 following for use in the port of Marin under the name *Remmar*.

The *Bargarth* was built by Richards (Shipbuilders) Ltd, Lowestoft, and launched on 5 April 1966 for service in South Wales. She is driven by a 850bhp Lister Blackstone main engine again with a single propeller located within a steerable Kort Nozzle. Her initial bollard pull of 14 tonnes was increased to 17 tonnes and her life extended in 1986 when she was fitted with a steerable Aquamaster retractable bow thruster unit giving her an additional 500bhp.

(Both photographs by Bernard McCall)

It is not always sunny when taking photographs of ships! On a bitterly cold winter morning, the **Bargarth** joins other members of the local Cory fleet in the lock at Cardiff on 19 January 1985, prior to bringing a large ship into port. Early in 2002, the tug was sold to owners based in Waterford and has been laid up there awaiting resale since that time.

(Bernard McCall)

The vast majority of tugs in this book are used for shiphandling and the **Towing Wizard** was certainly built as such. Typical of the output of German shipyards in the mid-1950s, she was built at the Mützelfeldwerft shipyard in Cuxhaven as the **Quaysider** for Tyne Tugs. Her Deutz engine of 1200bhp drives a single screw. In July 1984, following a period of lay-up in Sunderland, she joined the fleet of TSA Tugs Ltd and was renamed **Towing Wizard**. For the next decade, she was used in a much wider variety of work, mainly servicing coastal and deepsea towage contracts. It was work on such a contract which brought her to Barry on 13 June 1990. She was sold to Greek owners in 1994 and was renamed **Tora**.

(Bernard McCall)

14

The **Danegarth** was another of the class of attractive tugs built by Richards (Shipbuilders) Ltd, Lowestoft, in the mid-1960s. Launched on 7 February 1966 and originally operated by R & J H Rea, she passed with the company into Cory ownership in 1970. Her Blackstone engine delivers 850bhp; propulsion and power are identical to the **Bargarth** on pages 12/13. She was sold to Greek owners who renamed her **Linoperamata** and she left the Bristol Channel in February 1992. Evening lighting conditions were once again dramatic in South Wales as she assisted the reefer **Nickerie** as the latter departed from Barry on 21 October 1991.

(Bernard McCall)

A rather unexpected arrival in the Bristol Channel on 10 April 2003 was the Italian tug **Uran**. She was built in 1998 by Astilleros Armon at Navia and is powered by two Mak engines giving a total of 4080bhp and driving twin stern-mounted azimuthing propulsion units. This gives her a bollard pull of 50 tonnes. Owned by Ocean Srl, of Trieste, she is one of three tugs built for a specific contract in Trieste but this contract failed to materialise. She was chartered by Svitzer Marine Ltd following the transfer of the Bristol Channel tug **Shannon** to the Clyde fleet and prior to the arrival of the **Svitzer Bristol** (see page 9). During her stay in the Avonmouth fleet, she remained in her owner's colours but was renamed **Danegarth**. She left the Bristol Channel on 20 November 2003. The photograph shows her passing Barry at 8.00pm on 10 April 2003 as she made for Avonmouth for the first time.

(Chris Jones)

A similar view to this, but reproduced in monochrome, featured in the author's book *Tugs Around Britain*, published in 1992. No excuse is offered for reusing it because colour reproduction allows us to appreciate the full effect of the gentle evening light at the end of a fine spring day in Swansea. Furthermore, the tug has had an interesting history since 1992. The **Margam** was built for Alexandra Towing by Richard Dunston at Hessle and was launched on 17 August 1970. At the time, she was a state-of-the-art vessel. Although having only a single engine giving 2190bhp and a 40 tonne bollard pull, she had the unusual distinction of being fitted with a two-speed gearbox to provide optimum engine revolutions depending on whether she was towing or free running. She was considered ideal for handling tankers in Swansea's enclosed docks or bulk carriers at the exposed Port Talbot jetty which had its first caller on 8 January 1970. Indeed it was the latter vessels which she and sister tug **Mumbles** were specifically designed for. In early 1997, she was reported sold to Israeli interests but almost immediately was taken over by West Coast Towing who renamed her **Hurricane H** - and put her to work in exactly the same location as she had previous worked for rivals Howard Smith. The latter company was not impressed! Howard Smith withdrew from towage operations at Swansea on 9 October 1999, with Cory Towage moving in the following day.

(Bernard McCall)

During the mid-1990s, tug operations in South Wales and the Bristol Channel were challenged by the arrival in the area of a new company, West Coast Towing Co (UK) Ltd. Originally established in 1989, the company was remodelled in 1993 and a small tug fleet comprising four twin-screw tugs built in Russia was based in Newport. The first major contract was won in March when British Steel transferred from Alexandra Towing the work of handling large bulk carriers using the tidal jetties at Port Talbot. Expansion soon saw the company working throughout South Wales, and there were also visits to assist vessels being launched or on trials at Appledore. The speed of expansion is evidenced by the fact that the company owned fourteen tugs by autumn 1995. By 2001, however, harbour work was declining and the company's harbour towage operations were taken over by Wijsmuller Marine Ltd, which had already taken over West Coast's erstwhile competitors, Cory Towage. West Coast decided to concentrate on deepsea and offshore towage work.

Here we see the 1992-built *Capt I B Harvey*, a twin screw tug built at St Petersburg as *Vik III*. After construction, she was sold to Norwegian owners but remained unused and was laid up along with sistership *Vik IV* at Stavanger. The pair was towed to Newport where they arrived on 24 February 1994. Both are powered by two SKL engines giving 1600bhp and a bollard pull of 35 tonnes. The propulsion system is unique in British tugs, being controllable pitch propellers in Kort-type nozzles which are steerable and independently controlled. Although by no means the largest tug in the fleet, she has had important roles. In January 1998, she began work at the newly-opened Brussels Sea Canal after West Coast Towing had set up a joint enterprise with a local company; this was a first for any British tug owners.

(Danny Lynch)

As noted on the previous page, West Coast Towing won the contract to handle bulk carriers at Port Talbot in 1994 and two large tugs were bought from Portnet in South Africa to support this work. They were the **C M Hoffe** and **F H Boltman**, dating from 1977 and 1979 respectively and built in Durban by Dorman Long Vanderbijl Corporation Ltd. Previously working at Richards Bay, they would no doubt have assisted some of the bulk carriers which they were about to handle in Wales. The **C M**

Hoffe was renamed **Ryan** and her sistership became **Faris**. Their twin Mirrlees Blackstone engines, producing 4500bhp in total, drive twin controllable pitch propellers in Kort nozzles and they have a 53 tonne bollard pull. They were photographed in Svitzer livery at Swansea on 24 June 2003 when being readied to dock a bulk carrier at Port Talbot.

(Dominic McCall)

The **Argus T** was built i
Sweden in 1947. She has
single engine of 665bh
driving a controllable pitc
propeller. She had borne th
name **Fuerza** when purchase
and renamed **Argus T** b
owner Chris Thompson, o
Leigh-on-Sea, in 1980. In th
late 1980s, she was working a
Hartlepool but by early 198
was owned by Haven Service
Ltd and worked in Milfor
Haven. By summer 1990, sh
was providing towage service
at Grimsby.

Almost a whole book chapter would be needed to chart the history of these two tugs photographed together at Milford Haven on 29 August 1988. The **Dunheron** began life as the **Golden Cross** in the fleet of the Tees Towing Co Ltd, of Middlesbrough. A single-screw tug, she was built in 1955, being launched on 24 March that year at the Bowling yard of Scott & Sons. She is powered by a Crossley diesel engine of 750bhp driving a single screw and providing a modest 9 tonnes bollard pull. The tug's name commemorated the golden wedding in 1954 of Sir William and Lady Crossthwaite whose family had owned Tees Towing. In 1968, the **Golden Cross** was sold to the Newport Screw Towing Co Ltd in Newport, a company which would later become part of Cory Towage, and by whom she was renamed **Dunheron**. In late 1971, she was transferred to the Cory fleet in Belfast and was sold the following year to a Dublin company. After five years in Irish ownership from 1972, she entered the fleet of Carmet

Tugs Ltd and it is their funnel colours that she carries in this photograph. In 1991, she joined the fleet of Tyne Towage. By 1996 she was owned by Pounds Shipbreakers, Portsmouth, who sold her for use as a diving support vessel to work in the Philippines. This did not happen. Instead she was refurbished and restored to her original identity of **Golden Cross**. As such she had the distinction of assisting the Royal Yacht **Britannia** when the latter paid her final visit to London in November 1997. The tug had escorted the **Britannia** from the River Tees on 6 June 1956 when Her Majesty The Queen and the Duke of Edinburgh were departing on their first overseas visit in the ship. She currently works as a floating exhibition ship and at the time of writing is moored in Cardiff.

(Bernard McCall)

The **Millgarth** was the second of two tugs built at the Damen shipyard in Gorinchem. Like many vessels built on the continent, her hull was built at a different yard and was towed to Gorinchem for completion. In her case, the hull was launched at Gdansk on 28 September 1996 and construction at Gorinchem was completed on 19 February 1997. She arrived at Milford Haven four days later and entered service almost immediately. A stern drive tug of the Damen standard ASD 3211 design, her two Stork Wartsila engines deliver 5095bhp and drive twin stern-mounted multi-directional propellers rotating in fixed Kort nozzles. Sections of the maritime industry in the UK have sadly tended to cut themselves off from local communities so it was especially pleasing to see that the **Millgarth** and **Anglegarth** were formally named by local school children at a ceremony on 14 March. Here we see her assisting the German tanker **Dorsch** away from the Texaco terminal at Milford Haven on 24 May 2003.

(Bernard McCall)

On this page we find examples of three generations of tug[s] designed to assist large tankers in Milford Haven. Th[e] **Greengarth** was photographed in Milford dock on 27 Augu[st] 1986 and is an example of a third generation tug. She wa[s] launched on 9 March 1970 at the Hessle yard of Richa[rd] Dunston Ltd for R & J H Rea Ltd. Her 35 tonne bollard pull obtained from an English Electric engine of 2460bhp drivi[ng] a fixed-pitch propeller rotating in a steerable Kort nozzle. [In] 1993 she was sold to owners in Nigeria and was rename[d] **Real Support**.

The first generation of tugs is exemplified by the **Dalegar[th]** in the photograph below, taken on 31 July 1977.

(both photographs by Bernard McCa[ll]

The **Dalegarth** was built by Henry Scarr at Hessle and launched on 16 February 1960. Her British Polar engine of 1300bhp drives a fixed-pitch propeller and provides a bollard pull of 22 tonnes. Displaced from the Haven after the arrival of the G-class tugs in 1970, the **Dalegarth**, along with the **Anglegarth** and **Thorngarth**, left the Haven on 13 October 1970 to begin towage duties at the new Point Tupper oil refinery in Canada. Replaced at the Canadian refinery, she returned to Milford Haven in 1972 and was transferred to Avonmouth on 6 December 1977 and then was transferred to Newport in summer 1980 after the arrival of the **Point Gilbert** from Canada. In July 1984, she was sold to Falmouth Towage Ltd by whom she was renamed **St Piran**.

The **Exegarth** is one of four E-class tugs built for the Cory fleet at Milford Haven and representing the fourth generation. Launched on 17 May 1976 at the Beverley yard of the Drypool Shipbuilding Group, she had the dubious distinction of being the final vessel to be built at the yard. All four tugs in the class were named after rivers but the use of **Exegarth** and **Eskgarth** proved unfortunate as it caused VHF communication difficulties and the pilots and tug crews had to spell the first three letters of each tug's name for clarity. The **Exegarth**, along with sister tug **Eyegarth**, was sold for use at a coal terminal in the Philippines in mid-1995 and was renamed **Pagbilao I**. She has a Ruston engine of 3520bhp which drives a controllable pitch propeller rotating within a steerable Kort nozzle, this system giving a bollard pull of 50 tonnes.

24 July 1990 was a momentous day on Merseyside. The **Queen Elizabeth 2** anchored in mid-river and over a quarter of a million people lined the riverside to see her. She was escorted into the Mersey by tugs from both Cory and Alexandra fleets. In this view we see Cory's **Hollygarth** and **Willowgarth** providing a spectacular greeting. The **Hollygarth** was built by Appledore Shipbuilders in 1969, along with sister vessel **Brackengarth**. They were intended for handling the large tankers using Tranmere Oil Terminal and the Amlwch single-point buoy off the coast of Anglesey, their 50 tonne bollard pull being ideal for handling VLCCs. They are powered by two Ruston Hornsby engines of 3380bhp which drive a single controllable pitch propeller rotating in a steerable Kort nozzle. Launched as **Hollygarth** on 25 September 1969, the original intention had been to name her **Oakgarth**. She was sold in November 1996 to TSA Tugs by whom she was renamed **Towing Wizard**, replacing the tug of that name seen on page 14. The **Willowgarth** was built at Great Yarmouth by Richards (Shipbuilders) Ltd and launched on 21 April 1989. Her two Ruston engines of 3400 total bhp drive twin stern-mounted multi-directional propellers and provide a bollard pull of 45 tonnes.

(Bernard McCall)

The **Cedargarth** was a tug of pleasing design, built at the Appledore yard of P K Harris and launched on 10 October 1961. Her two Ruston Hornsby engines deliver 1300bhp and drive a single screw, giving a bollard pull of 18 tonnes. Her original owners were the Rea Towing Company Ltd, this becoming part of the Cory Ship Towage fleet in 1985. In 1992, she was sold to Tyne Towage which at the time was expanding its fleet. She was renamed **Mikey Dev**. The following year, she was bought by owners in the Somali Republic and sailed to Mogadiscio. Sharing the work of assisting a bulk carrier into Birkenhead is the **Beechgarth**, a tug of very similar design but built by W J Yarwood & Sons Ltd, Northwich, by whom she was launched on 7 January 1964. Her propulsion machinery is similar to that of the **Cedargarth** but her bollard pull of 19 tonnes is achieved by a slightly higher rated engine of 1430bhp. She was sold to UK owners in mid-1996 and renamed **Mounts Bay** and sold on in the same year being then renamed **Gym**, under which name she was berthed at Totnes for a while. In 1998, she was sold to Portuguese owners who renamed her **Roxanne**.

(Bernard McCall)

With the Cory fleet and its associate companies expanding rapidly in the 1970s and 1980s, new vessels were introduced as and when appropriate. The Mersey fleet of Rea Towing Co Ltd was the first to introduce a stern-mounted azimuthing propulsion system with the arrival from local builder McTay Marine Ltd of the **Eldergarth** and **Rowangarth**. They were the first tugs using Japanese propulsion equipment to be built in a British yard. Powered by two Niigata diesel engines with a total of 3300bhp, the **Rowangarth** has twin Z-Peller propulsion units in fully-rotating Kort nozzles. These are located beneath the stern of the tug, thus making her no deeper than a conventional tug. This system gives her a bollard pull of 42 tonnes ahead and an impressive 39 tonnes astern. When she entered service, she was registered in Westport, County Mayo, in the Republic of Ireland. In late November 1982, the **Rowangarth** and **Eldergarth** left the Mersey for a two-year spell of work at Cabinda in Angola. This was initially a two-year contract with the Chevron oil company but it was extended and other tugs have been sent over the years to replace the two original tugs. The **Rowangarth** was photographed at Eastham in April 1997. Just over two years later, she was transferred to the River Tyne.

(Bernard McCall)

On the same occasion as that shown on page 23, the **Herkules** was given the honour of handling the bow ropes of the **Queen Elizabeth 2**. This decision was not to everyone's liking because the tug was not in Alexandra colours, did not have an Alexandra name, and had only recently been chartered from Hapag-Lloyd. The charter had started in January 1990. Soon renamed **TS Herkules**, she remained on charter for a further four years and was eventually purchased in May 1994, by which time Alexandra Towing had been taken over by the Howard Smith group. She was then given the name **Gladstone**, a traditional Mersey tug name. Dating from 1977 when built at the Jadewerft shipyard, she worked in Bremen for Hapag-Lloyd. Her two MAK engines of 2400bhp drive a Voith Schneider propulsion unit and she has a bollard pull of 30 tonnes.

(Bernard McCall)

On 2 June 1966, the **B C Lamey** was launched at the Port Glasgow yard of James Lamont & Co Ltd for J H Lamey Ltd, tug operators on the Mersey since 1916. She was powered by a 1400bhp MWM engine of a design first fitted to the **William Lamey** some seven years earlier. What was notable was that the **B C Lamey** was the third tug for her owners to feature twin uptakes instead of a conventional funnel, thus giving the tug master better all-round vision. Again it was the **William Lamey** which had first featured this layout. The Lamey company had earned an enviable reputation for innovation in its Mersey tugs; these included VHF radio telephone, radar, fixed Kort nozzles - and indeed the motor tug. In July 1968, Alexandra Towing took over control of J H Lamey Ltd and the **B C Lamey** was renamed **Salthouse**. In 1975, she was transferred from her traditional Mersey base to Southampton, but she was evidently back on the Mersey when this photograph was taken on 12 August 1983. In early summer 1984, the **Salthouse** was sold to Larne-based J McLoughlin and was renamed **David F**. She had the misfortune to sink when assisting a ship at Londonderry on 16 June 1985 but was raised a week later. Though badly damaged, she was sold in 1986 to an owner in Devon and was repaired in Poole. Financial problems arose and the tug was then reported to be laid up in Milford Haven. By late 1987, she had been sold to Maltese owners and renamed **Zamtug II** but her problems continued when a floating crane, being towed on her delivery voyage, sank in the Irish Sea.

(Bernard McCall)

In many of my publications, I have expressed the view that the neglect of our commercial waterways over the last three decades has been nothing less than a national scandal. One such waterway is the Manchester Ship Canal; it is hard to imagine that other European countries would have allowed such a useful commercial artery to fade into such insignificance. The **M.S.C. Onward** was built by Henry Robb, Leith, in 1948, a time when the Canal was flourishing and when scarcely an hour would pass by without tugs moving along the Canal with ships in tow or to collect ships. She was a twin-screw tug powered by two Crossley engines which provided 1200bhp in total and was one of eight such tugs and was highly successful. She served the Canal until 1975 when she was sold to other UK owners and renamed *Fairlight* but almost immediately was renamed **Hastings**. Indeed she may never have borne the name *Fairlight*; certainly she never left port as such. There were rumours that she was to be used on contract work in the North Sea but in reality she was sold in 1976 to Piraeus-based operator Nicolas Vernicos by whom she was renamed **Triton**.

(John Slavin)

The **M.S.C. Viking** was the third of four identical tugs built for the Manchester Ship Canal Company by James Cook at Wivenhoe. She was launched on 19 January 1976. All four tugs have twin screws powered by two Allen diesel engines with a total of 1200bhp. On 7 March 1989, the Manchester Ship Canal Company announced that it was to contract out its towage operations on the canal and the work was taken over by Carmet Tugs which leased the four V-class tugs. Since the change, the tugs have been maintained in excellent condition, far better than in the final years of Canal Company operation. The **M.S.C. Viking** was photographed on 26 July 2001 as she assisted the Swedish tanker **Bro Axel** towards the lock at Eastham.

(Bernard McCall)

Built by Robert Cock at Appledore in 1906, it is no surprise that the diminutive **Primrose** had several owners during her long life. She was originally powered by a Sissons 35nhp steam reciprocating engine, she was converted to diesel in 1960 when fitted with a Ruston & Hornsby engine of 360bhp. An inland waterways tug, she was originally based in Gloucester and rarely ventured beyond Sharpness. However, two years after finishing work at Sharpness in 1979, she was bought by Peter Herbert and began to work in Devon and Cornwall. In 1983, she moved to work in Selby but was too big for the river here and she returned to Devon soon afterwards. In January 1985, she was sold to the Laxey Towing Co Ltd and it was during this company's ownership that she was photographed at Glasson Dock on 5 August 1985. She was often used to tow the former Bristol Channel barge **Sudbrook** to Manx ports laden with coal from Glasson Dock or Garston. She joined the Tyne Towage fleet in 1989 and was sold on to John Dean in Hull during 1991.

(Bernard McCall)

The preservation of seagoing vessels is a very attractive idea, at least emotionally, but many individuals and organisations fail to appreciate the huge costs involved. There are several preserved tugs to be seen around the UK - indeed we have already looked at two on page 4. The youngest tug to be preserved at the time of writing, and arguably the most active, is the *Brocklebank*, built in 1965 by W J Yarwood at Northwich for Alexandra Towing. Her Crossley engine of 1200bhp drives a single screw and provides an 18 tonne bollard pull. She served Alexandra on the Mersey, with occasional visits to Heysham and Barrow-in-Furness. She was also used to tow barges filled with stone from Dinmor Quarry on Anglesey to Liverpool for use in the building of Seaforth Dock.

She was withdrawn from service in 1988 and acquired the next year by the Merseyside Maritime Museum. Since then, she has been maintained in working order and regularly visits maritime festivals and similar events. As such, she has been a fine reminder of the once-familiar Alexandra colours in a wide variety of locations such as Douglas, Arklow, and here at Barrow-in-Furness on 17 August 2002. She also provides excellent publicity for the Friends of the Maritime Museum on these occasions.

(Bernard McCall)

Despite being involved in several takeovers, the **Thunderer**, photographed in the Clyde on 9 April 1986, spent much her life on that river apart from a time in the early 1990s on Ireland's west coast followed by a two-year spell in Belfast between 1993 and 1995. She was in fact constructed on the Clyde, her builder being James Lamont at Port Glasgow. Launched on 29 September 1969, she entered service in the fleet of Steel & Bennie Ltd as **Warrior**. Her owners became R & J H Rea Ltd in 1969 and then Cory Ship Towage in 1970. T & J Harrison had requested use of the name **Warrior** for a new vessel and so Cory agreed to rename its tug **Thunderer** in 1973. She eventually became one of a dying breed of single screw tugs and she was fortunate to survive into the new millennium. Despite her age and conventional propulsion system (Deutz engine of 2400bhp driving a fixed-pitch propeller in a steerable Kort nozzle), she was still able to deliver a bollard pull of 38 tonnes. She was sold to Spanish buyers in the Spring of 2003 and left the Clyde for the Canary Islands in April and was later renamed **Iron Bull**.

(Bernard McCall)

The tugs of the Port Auxiliary Service (PAS) and Royal Maritime Auxiliary Service (RMAS) have served in many naval ports over the years. In mid-1996, towage services operated by the RMAS in naval dockyards were taken over by Serco-Denholm, a consortium formed earlier in the year. The *Fiona* was based on the River Clyde when she was photographed on 30 July 1999 as she assisted the 1926-built sailing vessel *Kruzenshtern* during what has become popularly known as the Tall Ships Race. The tug was built at the Hancock shipyard, Pembroke Dock, in 1973. Her Mirrlees Blackstone engine of 615bhp drives a single Voith Schneider controllable pitch propeller and gives a bollard pull of 5.7 tonnes. At the time of writing, she is out of service because of engine problems and is offered for sale.

(Dominic McCall)

33

Like the **Point Gilbert** on the back cover, the **Point Spencer** was one of a group of tugs built at Richard Dunston's Hessle yard to work at the Come-by-Chance oil refinery in Newfoundland, Canada. She was launched on 10 August 1972. This tug and sister vessel **Point Carroll** differed from the first two tugs, **Point Gilbert** and **Point James**, in being fitted out for coastal and deepsea towage in addition to shiphandling. Towing winches were fitted and the tugs' hulls had a higher forecastle than the two earlier tugs. Propulsion in all tugs of the series was identical, namely a Ruston Paxman engine driving a single controllable-pitch propeller located in a steerable Kort nozzle but the output of the engines of the **Point Spencer** and **Point Carroll** was, at 3300bhp, higher than that of the other tugs. The **Point Spencer** returned from Canada to the UK in 1976 and, without a specific role in the Cory fleet, the company was able to utilise her coastal towing capabilities mainly in work on the east coast of England. By the early 1990s, the **Point Spencer** was based on the Clyde and she is seen here at the launch of the ferry **Isle of Lewis** at Port Glasgow on 18 April 1995. In early 2003, the tug was sold to Dutch owners and renamed **Hunter**.

(Bernard McCall)

Photographed at Greenock on 18 April 1995, the **Flying Phantom** was the last tug to wear the distinctive colours of Clyde Shipping. She was launched on 2 July 1981 by Ferguson Brothers Ltd at Port Glasgow and, as built, had a bollard pull of 35 tonnes. This was delivered by two Ruston main engines driving a single controllable pitch propeller rotating in a steerable Kort nozzle. She passed into the ownership of Cory Towage in 1995. Two years later she went to Dunston (Shiprepairers) Ltd, Hull, for extensive modifications, the most important of which being the fitting of a retractable Aquamaster fully-steerable azimuthing bow thruster unit. The tug was involved in a collision with a cargo ship on 29 December 2000. She was towed to drydock in Greenock later that day and subsequently repaired.

(Bernard McCall)

When the new oil export terminal at Sullom Voe in Shetland was being planned, it was decided that towage requirements would be in the hands of a new company, Shetland Towage Ltd in which Shetland Islands Council had a 50% share, Cory Ship Towage Ltd 25% and Clyde Shipping Ltd also 25%. The **Tystie** and **Dunter**, third generation tugs built for Shetland Towage Ltd for use at the Sullom Voe oil terminal on Shetland suffered a delay during construction when it was discovered that they were unable to achieve the specified astern bollard pull. The tugs were built by Ferguson Shipbuilders Ltd at Port Glasgow and this company, in conjunction with Voith Hydro Schiffstechnik, makers of the propulsion units, had to modify the blades of these units so that the tugs could meet the stringent requirements of the oil terminal's operators. The tugs are powered by two Caterpillar diesel engines each of 2720bhp and they have a bollard pull of 56 tonnes ahead. They are very sophisticated tugs being fully fitted not only for harbour towage but also for escort duty and emergency sea towage. Furthermore they have excellent firefighting and a self-protection drenching system. All of the tugs in the Shetland Towage fleet are named after Shetland sea birds, the **Dunter** being the eider duck. The impressive appearance of the tug is evident in this view of her going astern in Sullom Voe.

(David Dodds)

The mid-1990s saw a change in towage operations at the Hound Point tanker terminal from which BP exports its crude oil from the North Sea. By the end of 1996, towage operations were being handled by BP's own tugs following a gradual two-year changeover from tugs operated by Forth Tugs Ltd, an associate of Cory Towage Ltd, which had handled towage at the terminal since its inception in the mid-1970s. Three of the four original tugs are visible in this view dated 22 July 1983. Farthest from the camera is the **Kelty** while the **Boquhan** is nearest the camera and the **Duchray** in the middle. The latter two are firefighting vessels with high level monitors. All four have a bollard pull of 35 tonnes and their controllable pitch propellers located in a steerable Kort nozzle are driven by a single Ruston engine of 2640bhp. After ending their work at Hound Point, the tugs were laid up in Leith awaiting sale for several months from December 1996. The first to be sold was the **Boquhan** which, along with the **Duchray**, had been built at the Robb Caledon yard in Leith. She was the subject of a lease agreement to Divemex Ltd for use in supporting diving work at Conakry in West Africa, and was renamed **Oliver**. Purchase was completed two years later.

(Mike Hawkins)

Takeovers and mergers can be complex affairs and this was certainly the case in north-east England by the early 1980s when Lawson-Batey was the parent company of three fleets operating under separate names : Tyne Tugs Ltd, of Newcastle; France, Fenwick, Tyne & Wear Ltd, of Sunderland; and the Blyth Tug Company. With the rapid decline in shipbuilding and ship repairing in that part of England at the time, and a consequent reduction in tug requirements, a further rationalisation was inevitable and so in mid-1983, Lawson-Batey was taken over by the Clyde Shipping Company (Tugs) Ltd. The **Holmsider** was launched for the new company on 15 May 1984 at Richard Dunston's shipyard at Hessle and initially wore the attractive France, Fenwick Tyne & Wear funnel colours seen to advantage on page 40. Two years later, the original

Lawson-Batey funnel colours of golden ochre with a blue Maltese cross were applied to all the tugs within the group and are seen in this view dated April 1995. The **Holmsider** is powered by a Mirrlees Blackstone engine of 1125bhp driving a controllable pitch propeller located in a steerable Kort nozzle. In October 1997, the **Holmsider** was transferred to Newport and was renamed **Wyegarth**. Her stay was short-lived for in July 1998, she was sold to Stavros Karapiperis, of Piraeus, and renamed **Karapiperis 15**. This owner had already purchased other British tugs (see page 57).

(Harold Appleyard)

An unusual towage operation began on the River Tyne in May 1989 when colliery waste from Harton Colliery near the Tyne and Wearmouth Colliery at Sunderland was loaded into barges at riverside quays and then taken to sea for disposal. This method replaced disposal by powered hopper barges. The new system required the barges to be pushed and the initial work was undertaken by the **Weswear**, owned by North East Towing Ltd which was a subsidiary of Svitzer Towing, a large Danish company. This tug had been converted for pusher use and had been transferred from Svitzer's harbour fleet in Copenhagen. She was occasionally supplemented by the **Mjølner** from Svitzer's own fleet. which was photographed pushing a barge on the Tyne in April 1989. She was built in 1974 at the Kristiansand S yard of P Høivolds Mek Verksted, and was refurbished at Skagen in January 1989. Her Alpha diesel engine of 3150bhp drives a controllable pitch propeller and gives a bollard pull of 32 tonnes.

(Harold Appleyard)

We have referred elsewhere to the difficulties experienced by smaller tug companies which set up business to compete against larger, well-established companies. On Tyneside, the locally-based Tyne Towage expanded quickly in the early 1990s and undertook coastal towing and civil engineering contacts in addition to shiphandling. One acquisition in 1992 was the former Avonmouth tug **Pengarth** which had had three owners since her disposal by Cory in February 1991. She was first sold shortly after the arrival of the **Avongarth** (see page 6). Having a bollard pull of 14.5 tonnes and powered by a Ruston Hornsby engine of 1080bhp driving a single screw, she was built by Charles Hill Ltd, Bristol, for R & J H Rea in 1962 and was launched on 14 August that year. She was sold by Tyne Towage in early 1997 and departed from the UK for new owners in West Africa. Based in Togo, she was renamed **Vigilant**. The photograph was taken on 11 April 1994.

(Michael Green)

The **Whitburn** has the distinctive appearance of one of the very many tugs built during the Second World War in the USA. Dating from 1943, she was a product of the American Shipbuilding Corporation and her General Motors engine delivered 700bhp. After the War, she was sold to Norwegian owners for use in Bergen and she came to the UK when bought by France, Fenwick, Tyne & Wear Co Ltd. Renamed **Whitburn**, she gave valiant service at Sunderland until sold to Egyptian owners in Port Said in the spring of 1978. She left Hull for Egypt on a pontoon barge on 17 April that year. She was coming to the end of her career at Sunderland when photographed in the port on 25 August 1976.

(Michael Green)

Though not the oldest tug in this book, the **Pallion** has an interesting history. She was built in 1944 by Richard Dunston, Thorne, as the **TID 172** and bore the name **Evelyn** for a while. In 1948, she was purchased by the then River Wear Commissioners and was used mainly to handle the port's dredging equipment. As part of a refit in 1972, she was re-engined with a Lister Blackstone engine of 405bhp which replaced a steam engine of 220ihp. She is seen at Sunderland on a sunny January day in 1988.

(Harold Appleyard)

As her name suggests, the **Seaham Pride** is normally based at Seaham Harbour and it is here that she was photographed on 9 April 1989. She is occasionally hired to other ports on the east coast for towage and plough dredging duties. She is a Damen standard tug and was built in 1975. She is powered by two General Motors engines each of 360bhp and has a bollard pull of 7.2 tonnes. She was bought from Scottish owners in 1982 and had previously been named **Boy Henry**. She was delivered from Glasgow to Seaham via the Crinan Canal and Caledonian Canal.

(Michael Green)

In the late 1950s and early 1960s, many examples of tugs were built with a hull design known as hydroconic. Some of these were built at the yard of P K Harris Ltd in Appledore. The **Stranton** and sister vessel **Hart**, were built in 1958 for service in the port of Hartlepool. Both were twin-screw tugs powered by Lister Blackstone main engines of 1200bhp in total and were withdrawn from service in June 1995 when Cory took over responsibility for towage in Hartlepool. The **Stranton**, seen here at Hartlepool in 1987, was sold to Bilberry Shipping & Stevedoring, of Waterford, on 1 November 1995. Three years later, the tug was sold to civil engineering contractors in Lebanon and departed for Beirut flying the Cambodian flag.

(Harold Appleyard)

We now move to the southern bank of the River Tees where we see the oddly-named **Samurai Swordsman** at work in February 1992. Very much a north-east tug, she was originally named **Wearsider** and worked for Tyne & Wear Tugs on the rivers from which the owning company was named. Built by Richard Dunston at Hessle in 1980, she is a single screw tug of 1125bhp, her engine being a Mirrlees Blackstone. On trials, she achieved a bollard pull of 17 tonnes. She entered service for Lawson Batey Tugs Ltd. She was transferred to Blyth in late 1983. In 1990, however, she was chartered to North Sea Tugs Ltd and worked on the River Thames, unusually pushing barges. Then in 1991, she was employed on the River Tees mainly assisting Japanese car carriers, hence her distinctive name. In 1992, she reverted to the name **Wearsider** and was sold five years later to Greek owners by whom she was renamed **Megalohari VI**.

(Harold Appleyard)

The Tees Towing Company Ltd was formed in 1920 following the amalgamation of the two major tug operators on the River Tees at the time. The new company was in the hands of the Crosthwaite family who began to use the suffix "Cross" on their tug names in 1927. During the ensuing half century, the company became renowned for its innovative approach. It introduced the first diesel-electric tug for shiphandling in Europe, the first tug with direct bridge control of engines, the first tug with hydraulic towing gear (all in 1933), the first tug built in the UK with a Kort nozzle (1957), and the first rudder-propeller tug in the UK (1976).

Photographed in what was once the familiar setting of Middlesbrough Dock on 14 April 1977, the **Marton Cross** (left) was built by Richard Dunston, Hessle, in 1963. Her Crossley diesel engine of 1125 bhp drove a single screw and a Kort nozzle helped to give her a bollard pull of 17 tons. In June 1981, she was sold to Willem Muller, of Terneuzen, by whom she was renamed **Waasland**. This company has purchased several tugs from the Tees fleet.

(Michael Green)

March 1974 saw the arrival on the River Tees of a new tug of revolutionary appearance. Built at the Richards yard in Great Yarmouth, the **Ralph Cross** had two small funnels instead of the usual large single funnel and an all-glass wheelhouse rather than conventional wheelhouse and flying bridge. Although of radical appearance, she retained conventional propulsion, being powered by a Ruston engine of 2640bhp driving a single screw in a Kort nozzle, giving her a bollard pull of 42 tonnes. She is seen on the outside of this view. She was sold to Maltese owners in July 1989 and renamed **Grez**.

In the centre is the **Norton Cross**, launched at Dunston's Hessle yard on 20 March 1984. She has two Ruston engines of 3400 total bhp which drive Aquamaster azimuthing propulsion units, giving 43 tonnes bollard pull. She was transferred to the River Mersey in May 1994.

Adjacent to the wharf is the **Eston Cross**, an identical sister to the **Norton Cross** and delivered in April 1985. In January 1994, she was transferred to Milford Haven and five months later was renamed **Stackgarth**. This was the first of a series of moves. 1997 saw her transferred to the Mersey, then to Belfast and finally back to Liverpool. On 9 October 1998, she had the honour of beginning Cory work at Swansea after the departure of Howard Smith tugs. During the summer of 1999, she transferred up the Bristol Channel to join the fleet based at Avonmouth and then underwent several mechanical and structural modifications to improve performance and visibility. The photograph is dated 18 April 1985.

(Michael Green)

Launched at Richard Dunston's Hessle shipyard on 24 May 1979, the **Yarm Cross** was completed three months later. Having a bollard pull of 35.5 tonnes, she is powered by two Ruston diesel engines with a total of 2640bhp. This drydock view shows her two azimuthing multi-directional propellers. In fact, the drydock is in Hull and the photograph was taken in August 1979 prior to her delivery to the Tees. She remains at work in north-east England but has latterly been based on the River Tyne.

(Harold Appleyard)

In September 1990, Tees Towing Ltd was taken over by Cory and various liveries were tried in an attempt to display the identity of the new owners whilst retaining vestiges of the old. Most were unsuccessful. Certainly the Cory diamond imposed on the Tees Towing funnel of the **Cleveland Cross**, photographed on 12 January 1991, is less than satisfactory. The Hessle-built tug was launched at Richard Dunston's yard on 18 September 1989 and completed just of one month later. She has twin Ruston main engines of 3440bhp in total driving twin Voith Schneider propellers and providing a bollard pull of 37 tonnes. She has now been transferred further north than the **Yarm Cross** for she is working at Grangemouth on the Forth of Forth at the time of writing.

(Michael Green)

We move south along England's eastern coast to the River Humber and its tributary, the River Ouse. Most of the towage activity takes place in the lower reaches of the Humber in the ports of Hull, Grimsby and Immingham. However, there is an occasional need for tugs to go upriver and into the Ouse. That need has diminished considerably since the closure of the shipbuilding yards in Goole and Selby. It was to the latter yard that the 1967-built **Lady Laura** was bound when she was photographed on a warm May evening in 1988. She was built at the Lowestoft yard of Richards (Shipbuilders) Ltd and is powered by two Ruston & Hornsby engines providing 1240bhp in total and a 16 tonne bollard pull. In 2000, she was sold to Briggs Commercial Ltd, based in Leith, and was renamed **Forth Drummer**. She was fitted with a new towing winch to make her more suitable for use in the work of her new owners.

(Roy Cressey)

Having taken over the fleet of Alexandra Towing in the early 1990s, the Howard Smith group ordered new state-of-the-art tugs and once these were delivered in mid-decade, older tugs were sold or redeployed. The **Ganges** had the distinction of being the final single screw tug built for Alexandra Towing (Felixstowe) Ltd and was launched on 23 February 1982. She is seen on 7 March 1982 during the final stages of fitting out at the Richard Dunston shipyard in Hessle. Propulsion is a controllable pitch propeller which rotates in a steerable Kort nozzle and is driven by a Ruston diesel engine of 2640bhp. Registered at London when launched, this was changed to Harwich before delivery to work in the Haven ports. By coincidence, she was displaced from Felixstowe in the autumn of 1996 and moved south to work in the Thames. A different coincidence saw her transferred back to the river where she was built for she moved to the Humber in late 2003.

(Bernard McCall)

The Dunston yard at Hessle had a long tradition of building tugs for the Ministry of Defence. It is of note, therefore, that the **Impulse** and sister vessel **Impetus** were the last tugs to be built by the yard for British ownership. They were delivered in 1993 and the yard closed at the end of that year. These were significant tugs not only because of their history but also because of their purpose. They were to be used for handling submarines, especially **Trident**-class submarines, berthing at the Clyde Submarine Base at Faslane and as they underwent trials in the Firth of Clyde. This interesting view shows the **Impetus** on the slipway at Hessle and clearly evident is the substantial fendering below the waterline to minimise contact with submarines when manoeuvring at close quarters. The **Impetus** was launched on 8 February 1993, five days after this photograph was taken. She has two Aquamaster fully azimuthing rudder/propeller units positioned beneath the stern and these are powered by two Allen main engines which deliver 3400bhp. Bollard pull ahead is 38.6 tonnes.

(Michael Green)

In 1973, the fleets of Grimsby-based J H Pigott & Sons and Hull-based United Towing Ltd were merged to become Humber Tugs Ltd. In 1977, this company became part of the North British Maritime Group and this in turn was taken over by the Howard Smith Group, an Australian company, ten years later. At the time, Howard Smith announced that it was to use the takeover as a step to expanding its operations in the UK. The results of this promise are evident on many pages of this book.

The **Lady Constance** was launched at the Selby yard of Cochrane Shipbuilders Ltd on 12 January 1982. Her two Ruston engines deliver a total of 2640bhp and drive two Voith Schneider propulsion units, this combination providing a 32 tonne bollard pull. She is seen assisting the **Forthbank** towards the lock at Hull on 22 October 1995.

(Bernard McCall)

During the 1990s, John Dean built up an interesting fleet of varied second-hand tugs. Here we see the **Shovette**, more details of which will be found on page 63. Here we comment on her propulsion system which was designed to maximise performance in pull or push mode. She has two Caterpillar diesel engines each of 360bhp which drive a pair of Schottel omnidirectional screw propellers able to provide thrust throughout 360° and providing a bollard pull of 10 tonnes. Thus sideways manoeuvrability is also excellent. The tug was launched as a bare hull and then was mounted on a cradle before being hauled back onto a slip so that underwater components could then be fitted. She is seen here pushing a LASH barge in the River Humber on 30 October 2003.

(Dominic McCall)

The pusher tug **Freight Endeavour** is a type of vessel very common on the canals and large rivers of northern Europe and the USA but relatively rare in the UK. She was built for the Port of London Authority in 1967 and was originally named **Placer**. After only seven years service, she was sold to the British Waterways Board for use on the Humber as part of the BACAT (Barge Aboard Catamaran) system. This worked on a principle very similar to the LASH system. The tug was converted for this purpose. She eventually entered John Dean's fleet in 1990. She is seen in the Hull dock system on 8 March 1997.

(Roy Cressey)

From the mid-1980s onwards, domestic shipyards in the UK have closed and there has been a corresponding increase in the number of tugs built elsewhere in Europe or even further afield. The **Lady Stephanie** was one of a pair of tugs built at the Argibay shipyard, Alverca, in Portugal and delivered in Spring 1984. Ironically they were based on a highly successful design for two tugs delivered two years previously by the Cochrane yard at Selby. Her two Ruston diesel engines of 2640bhp in total drive twin Voith Schneider units and provide a 32 tonne bollard pull. The **Lady Stephanie** is seen in the lock at Immingham providing stern assistance to the Cypriot freighter **Titan** on 14 October 1989.

(Roy Cressey)

In 1990, Humber Tugs Ltd, now a subsidiary of the Howard Smith group, placed an order with McTay Marine Ltd, Bromborough, for five new tugs valued at a total of £15 million. This was believed to be the largest order ever placed by a UK company for new tugs. The **Lady Sarah** was the third of the five to be delivered. Like her four sister vessels, the **Lady Sarah** is powered by twin Ruston diesel engines of 4600bhp in total driving twin Voith Schneider propulsion units and providing a bollard pull of 56 tonnes.

As she heads into the Humber from Immingham, the tug looks resplendent in the colours of Adsteam (UK) Ltd which had taken over Howard Smith Towage in May 2001 and in so doing became part of the largest independent harbour towage operator in the world with 156 tugs at the time of the takeover.

(Roy Cressey)

Another towage service has been offered at Grimsby by Survey & Supply since the mid-1990s. The company currently operates four tugs, one of these being the *Jadi*, acquired in 1996. She is a vessel of typical German appearance and previously worked at Bremen as **Butjadingen**. She was built at the Jadewerft yard in Wilhelmshaven. Her Deutz engine of 1300bhp provides a bollard pull of 11.5 tonnes. She was photographed off the port entrance at Grimsby on 4 October 2003.

(Roy Cressey)

From 1 January 1991, tugs of the Alexandra Towing fleet began to handle ships in Tilbury Dock, thus making the PLA's tugs redundant. The last two of these, the tractor tugs **Plasma** and **Platoon** were purchased by Alexandra and given extensive refit at Sheerness. They emerged with names revived from the William Watkins fleet, the **Plasma** being renamed **Burma** and the **Platoon** becoming **Dhulia**.

They moved to Swansea and were given local names **Langland** and **Caswell**. Their next move saw them transferred from Swansea to Grimsby in January 1998 and they were then given the traditional Humber names of **Lady Joan** and **Lady Theresa**. They are seen here in Grimsby on 27 March 1999. The tugs were purchased by Survey & Supply in 2001 and renamed **Joan** and **Lady**. Both were built at Richard Dunston's Hessle shipyard. They have a 14 tonne bollard pull.

(Roy Cressey)

Early in 2003, SMS Towage Ltd announced that it was to form a tug fleet in order to offer towage services in the Humber estuary, thus making four companies providing such services. On 16 June 2003, SMS bought a small tug from Norway which it felt was ideal for use on the Humber. The **Riverman** was photographed on 4 October 2003 when off Grimsby. She is an example of a standard design from builder AS Haugesunds Slip and powered by two GB Detroit diesel engines each of 210bhp. She was delivered in September 1977 as **Skorpo**. Ownership changed in 1990 but the most significant event in her career came in December 1992 when she was transferred to the Royal Norwegian Navy for use at the Haakonsvern naval base in Bergen as **VSD 10 Bogøy**. On 10 June 2003, she reverted to civilian ownership when acquired by a Bergen owner for resale and was briefly renamed **Skorpo**. Within a week she was deleted from the Norwegian register following purchase by SMS.

(Roy Cressey)

The **Brightwell** is seen off Felixstowe as she makes fast to an inbound container ship off the port entrance on 2 May 1988. Built at the Great Yarmouth yard of Richards Shipbuilders Ltd and launched on 25 June 1986, she was the first stern-drive tug using twin Aquamaster azimuthing propulsion units to appear in the Alexandra Towing fleet. Her twin Ruston diesel engines deliver 3444bhp and provide a bollard pull of 41.2 tonnes. She gave five years of excellent service to ships using Felixstowe but was transferred from the port to Southampton in April 1991 following the arrival of the **Trimley** which we see on the next page. During 2003, however, she returned to Felixstowe.

(Bernard McCall)

Built like the **Brightwell** by Richards Shipbuilders Ltd at Great Yarmouth for Alexandra Towing, the **Trimley** was launched on 6 December 1990 and was handed over to her owners on 15 March 1991. She is a stern-drive tug with a bollard pull of 44 tonnes. Her two Ruston main engines produce a total of 3860bhp and they drive twin Aquamaster azimuthing propulsion units. The familiar buff/white/black Alexandra colours did not suit her slender funnels and she looked far better in the Howard Smith colours as seen in this view at Felixstowe on 12 April 1998.

(Ian Willett)

Felixarc Marine Ltd provided workboats and tugs and mooring services in the Felixstowe area for many years. In the spring of 2001, it was announced that the company had been bought by Howard Smith (UK) Ltd at about the same time that the latter company was itself being taken over by Adsteam Marine Ltd [later branded Adsteam (UK) Ltd] as reported on page 51. The **Gray Alpha** is a typical Damen standard tug/workboat and was built at the Damen yard in Sliedrecht in 1985. She is a twin-screw vessel with General Motors engines producing 730bhp. In mid-2001, the tug was sold to Dredging International.

(Ian Willett)

The **Gary Gray**, photographed on 28 May 1979, was based on England's east coast for the early part of her life. She was built in 1954 by P K Harris at Appledore as **Jaycee** for service on the River Thames. She is powered by a Lister Blackstone engine of 360bhp. In February 1962, she was sold to United Towing who renamed her **Lighterman**. In September 1977, the **Lighterman** was sold to Felixarc Marine Ltd and she was renamed **Gary Gray**. The next stage in her career saw her move away from the south-east of England for she was sold to owners based at Heysham in mid-1988. She worked locally without change of name until 1995 when she had the misfortune to sink at her moorings and she became a total loss.

(Bernard McCall)

The **Sauria** was yet another product of the once-prolific Richard Dunston yard at Hessle and was launched on 27 May 1968. She was built for Gaselee and Sons (Felixstowe) Ltd before the company's takeover by Alexandra Towing. She was photographed at Ipswich on 2 June 1982. A little over two years later, on 30 July 1984, she collided with a Cuban ship which she was escorting into Felixstowe and was pushed over. Thankfully none of her crew was injured, though some had to leap into the water. She herself suffered serious damage but was repaired and put back into service. Displaced by the **Brightwell**, the **Sauria** moved to Swansea early 1987. There she was prepared for sale and later in the year she was bought by Greek owner Stavros Karapiperis by whom she was renamed **Karapiperis VI**.

(Bernard McCall)

The **Cobham** and sister vessel **Shorne** were built by McTay Marine Ltd, Bromborough, for the Dover Harbour Board and were named **Dextrous** and **Deft** originally. They each have two Ruston engines giving 2800 bhp in total and these drive twin Voith Schneider units. A bollard pull of 30 tonnes was achieved on trials. The tugs were designed to assist ferries to berth and unberth in poor weather conditions and a notable feature is the large stern with a heavy fender. This was needed to allow for the rubbing strakes of the ferries which varied in height. The **Cobham** was photographed in the River Thames at Dartford as she assisted the tanker **Wels** on 14 October 2001.

(Dominic McCall)

The **Sun Sussex** was launched on 5 May 1992 at the Great Yarmouth yard of Richards Shipbuilders Ltd, and was delivered to Alexandra Towing on 24 July that year. She and sister vessel **Sun Surrey** are each powered by two Ruston diesel engines producing a total of 3860bhp and driving two Voith Schneider propulsion units. They have a 43 tonne bollard pull. On 8 April 2001, the **Sun Sussex** was photographed as she assisted the container ship **New Zealand Pacific** into Tilbury Dock .

(Ian Willett)

Of course, takeovers and mergers have always happened in the towage industry as in any other industry. On 1 January 1975, Alexandra Towing took over London Tugs Ltd. This company had been formed in 1969 when W H J Alexander & Co Ltd, owners of Sun Tugs, merged with Ship Towage (London) Ltd. This company itself had been established in 1950 by the merger of William Watkins Ltd and The Elliott Steam Tug Company (1949) Ltd and the acquisition of Gamecock Tugs Ltd. The **Sun II** was built in 1965 for W H J Alexander & Co Ltd by C D Holmes Ltd, Beverley. She and sister vessel **Sun III** were open for public inspection in the Pool of London on 3 May 1966. She spent her whole life on the Thames until sold to Greek owners in autumn 1992, sailing from Sheerness to Chalkis on 12 October. The arrival on the Thames in 1977 of the **Sun Essex**, along with **Sun Kent** and **Sun London**, introduced a new style of name, maintaining the Sun prefix but adding a location rather than a Roman numeral.

The **Sun Essex** was also a product of a Humberside yard, namely that of Richard Dunston at Hessle where she was launched on 22 March 1977. She was the first in a series of three tugs, the **Sun Kent** being identical but the **Sun London** having a higher engine rating and no fire monitors. The **Sun Essex** has a Ruston Paxman engine of 2070bhp driving a controllable pitch propeller located in a steerable Kort nozzle. This arrangement gives a bollard pull of 32 tonnes. She is also fitted with a towing winch to allow coastal tows. In early 1990, she was transferred to Southampton, becoming the first fully-equipped firefighting tug to be located there by Alexandra Towing. Sold in 2000 to Norwegian owners, she was renamed **Big**, later being purchased by Danish interests and renamed **Susanne A** in 2002. The **Sun II** and **Sun Essex** were photographed as they passed Northfleet on 26 September 1987.

(Ian Willett)

Leaving Tilbury on 14 January 2001 is the **Towing Diamond**, a powerful tug with a varied history. Built in 1973 by P Holvolds Mek Verksted, Kristiansand S, for Norwegian owners, she was originally named **Aiolos.** She was sold to Greece five years later and became **Tinos** but returned to northern Europe in 1991 when bought by Lowestoft-based Klyne Tugs for whom she worked until 1994 as **Anglian Salvor**. She then returned to Norwegian ownership and was renamed **Master Mammut** but was purchased by TSA Tugs Ltd, of Leigh-on-Sea, early in 1998 to replace the company's **Towing Witch** which had been lost by fire. She has two Normo main engines which provide 5600bhp and drive a controllable pitch propeller located in a fixed Kort nozzle. She has a bollard pull of 70 tonnes when using both engines. The new millennium started badly for her owners and they ceased trading in January 2002. Eventually the **Towing Diamond** was sold to owners based in the Mediterranean and after a period laid up at Tilbury, she left under the name **Diamond** in tow for Gibraltar during October 2003.

(Ian Willett)

The **Horton** was built at Richard Dunston's Thorne yard in 1968 for ship handling in the port of Blyth. She has a single screw in a Kort nozzle which was driven originally by a Kelvin diesel engine of 240bhp. In the early summer of 1975, she moved to the west coast of England when purchased for handling trawlers at Fleetwood but she moved back to the east coast in 1979 when bought by Thames-based owners by whom she was renamed **D A McCann**. In 1986 she was purchased by A W Marine Services, of Leigh-on-Sea in Essex, and was usually to be found working on civil engineering contracts in the Rivers Thames and Medway, and off the south coast of England. In mid-1997, her original Kelvin engine was replaced by a more powerful Kelvin unit of 440bhp. This modification necessitated a change of gearbox also. She was photographed as she made her way down the River Medway in Rochester on 10 July 1999.

(Bernard McCall)

The **Shovette** and near sister **Lashette** were built at the Strood yard of the London & Rochester Trading Co Ltd for that company's own account. The **Lashette** came first, built in 1972, followed two years later by the **Shovette** which was in fact named **Grey Lash** until 1983 because she was built for an associated company, Humphrey & Grey Ltd. Both were used for what was at the time the innovative LASH (Lighter Aboard Ship) system, with lighters/barges being floated off larger ships after a transatlantic voyage and then taken by tug directly to another wharf for discharge. Fine in theory because of the reduction in handling, the system failed to find the popularity which it deserved. The reasons for the failure were political, the system arriving in the UK at a time of considerable industrial unrest and dockers foresaw a loss of employment. However, the tugs were not sold until mid-1998, the **Shovette** finding work handling commercial ships using the port of Chatham after the Royal Navy had left the port in 1983. The **Lashette** was sold to John Dean Tugs in Hull and the **Shovette** was sold along with the remainder of the former London & Rochester company's towage business to Deutsche Binnenreederei (UK) Ltd. The **Shovette** has a conventional bow and a stern designed for pushing with "push-knees". She was photographed in the River Medway on 10 July 1999.

(Bernard McCall)

The arrival in the Medway of the **Lady Emma** on 9 September 1998 ended a few months of intense activity by Howard Smith (UK) Ltd.The company had already decided that extra capacity was needed on the Medway when it discovered that a newly-built tug was available in Hong Kong. The **Chek Chau** was one of a pair of tugs delivered to Hong Kong Salvage & Towage Co Ltd by the Imamura Shipbuilding Company, of Kure, Japan, at the start of 1998. After only a few months in service for her owners in the Far East, she was bought in July 1998 by Howard Smith and delivered under her own power. After arrival in the Medway, she was drydocked at Chatham where some modifications were made. Also, the letter H was added to her name as another vessel on the UK register already had the name **Lady Emma**. Powered by two Niigata main engines giving 3600bhp in total, she has twin Niigata fully-azimuthing propulsion units and claims a bollard pull of 49.7 tonnes. She was photographed with the **Lady Brenda** alongside the car carrier **Tagus** at Sheerness on 10 July 1999, prior to assisting the large vessel from the berth.

(Bernard McCall)

The Medway-based company of J P Knight has the distinction of being the oldest family-owned towage company in Britain, having started in 1892. Its tugs, with familiar black funnels bearing a white letter K, were once a common sight on the Medway but are now no longer seen there. They are, however, seen in Scotland where associated company J P Knight (Caledonian) Ltd operates tugs in the Cromarty Firth but they have several important overseas contracts, notably in Surinam and Guyana. Never afraid to innovate, the company has the distinction of introducing the first stern drive Japanese-built tug to northern Europe when the *Kinross* arrived in 1981. In 1985, the company purchased a new tug which was being built by Hanasaki Zosensho in Yokosuka. This tug was launched as *Yokosuka Maru No. 2* on 3 June 1985 but was completed later that month as *Kenley* for J P Knight (Rochester) Ltd. The autumn of 1987 found her at work on the Mersey when she had been chartered by Rea Towage Ltd to cover for a period when this company's own tugs were drydocked or deployed elsewhere. In June 1991, J P Knight (Rochester) Ltd was taken over by the Howard Smith group and a new company was formed, Medway Towage Ltd, which was a wholly-owned subsidiary of Humber Tugs Ltd. Soon after this takeover, the five-strong Medway fleet was repainted in Howard Smith livery and the *Kenley* was renamed *Lady Brenda*. She subsequently came into the Adsteam fleet and it is this livery she wears in this photograph taken when she was awaiting an inbound vessel off Sheerness on 15 June 2003.

(Bernard McCall)

The **Meeching** was constructed at the Appledore yard of P K Harris for the port of Newhaven in 1960. She is another excellent example of the "hydroconic" hull design which was popular for British tugs at the time (see page 42 for a further example). She is powered by two Lister Blackstone engines with a combined output of 1320bhp which drive twin screws, achieving a bollard pull of 14 tonnes. Early in 2000 she was sold by Sea Containers, by then owners of Newhaven port, to other UK owners who placed her under the management of a Newhaven company but she has worked over a much wider area than the south coast port since her sale. She was photographed when sporting one of the Sealink liveries at Newhaven on 9 July 1986.

(Bernard McCall)

The community-conscious port of Shoreham arranges an Open Day every two years. Tours through the port are offered on this occasion and one vessel used is the port's tug, **Adurni**. She was photographed conveying a group of visitors during the Open Day in July 1998. The tug was delivered by her builder, Delta Shipyards, of Sliedrecht, early in 1984. She is a standard tug of a type designated Delta Tug 15-75. She has two Detroit Diesel main engines of 720bhp in total and these drive twin screws. Her 10 tonne bollard pull is quite adequate for handling ship's in the port area.

(Bernard McCall)

During the 1980s, there was a significant increase in the number and size of commercial ships using Portsmouth harbour. In 1983, local company J Butcher & Sons Ltd acquired its first purpose-built tug. This company, providing harbour trips around the dockyard and workboats for commercial ships, had traditionally used such boats as tugs so the addition of a small tug fleet was a natural extension of its business. The commercial dock area in Portsmouth can take ships up to 172 metres long yet is in an awkward location so compact but powerful tugs are needed. The **Jack**

James is the newest addition to the fleet, having arrived in Portsmouth on 6 September 2002. She is a Damen Stan Tug 1605 design and has the most powerful propulsion system of any of the tugs so far built to this design. Her two Caterpillar engines produce 1080bhp in total and drive two fixed-pitch propellers rotating in Van de Giessen nozzles. This system gives a bollard pull of 14.5 tonnes. The photograph was taken on 20 September 2003.

(Bernard McCall)

In early summer 1993, it was announced that a 10-year contract for the provision of towage, escort and anti-pollution duties at Esso's Fawley terminal on Southampton Water had been awarded to Solent Towage Ltd, a new company which was a wholly-owned subsidiary of Johannes Østensjø, of Haugesund, Norway, a company which has come to specialise in providing tugs for towage, escort duties, rope handling and pollution control duties at oil terminals. To service the contract, the company initially chartered two new Italian tugs, **Algerina Neri** and **Tito Neri**. These were soon replaced by two purpose-built tugs, the **Thrax** and **Silex**, sisterships each having a bollard pull of 60 tonnes. They were built in 1994 at Flekkefjord and they are powered by two Wartsila engines giving a total of 5386bhp. The pair are seen at Fawley on 7 June 2003 along with the small 1993-built tug/workboat **Ibex** which herself has a 7.8 tonne bollard pull.

(Bernard McCall)

During the latter part of the last millennium, towage at Southampton was dominated by two companies, one of these being the Southampton, Isle of Wight & South of England Royal Mail Steam Packet Co Ltd, better (and more simply!) known as Red Funnel. Illustrating that company's fleet is the 1979-built **Clausentum**, a product of the Lowestoft yard of Richards Shipbuilders Ltd. Two Ruston diesel engines deliver 2820bhp and drive twin controllable pitch propellers rotating in Kort nozzles, giving a bollard pull of 37 tonnes. The tug was photographed in Southampton Water on 24 August 1986. In the summer of 1993, she was sold to the Londonderry Port and Harbour Commissioners and was renamed **Strathfoyle**. In 2001, the tug was chartered to Norwegian owners for eight months but a purchase option was not exercised. Early in 2002, her owners decided to withdraw from tug ownership and the tug was sold to the Svendborg Towing Co Ltd in Denmark. She was renamed **Westsund** and was to be used principally on charter work involving the delivery of the hulls of new vessels for completion in various north European shipyards.

(Bernard McCall)

In the 1990s, the Red Funnel tugs were given a red hull but this hardly enhanced their appearance. The **Gatcombe** was one of a pair of tugs built in 1970 to handle the tankers visiting Esso's huge oil terminal at Fawley on Southampton Water. She was a single screw tug of 4,500bhp, fitted with a steerable Kort nozzle, and having a 35 tonne bollard pull. Because of her work with tankers, she was equipped with fire monitors. In addition to those on the wheelhouse roof, she had a Simon Snorkle elevating monitor platform which could direct a water jet from 30 metres above the waterline. Commonly seen on road-based fire tenders, such equipment was rare on tugs. She and sister tug **Vecta** were on station permanently at Fawley until it was decided in 1991 that the presence of an escort tug was needed. A Swedish tug, the **Portunus**, was chartered and the **Gatcombe** was transferred to the Southampton port fleet. As noted on page 69, the contract for providing towage services at Fawley was transferred from Red Funnel to Solent Towage in 1993. She was photographed at Netley Anchorage on 10 September 1994. Early in 1997, she was sold to Multraship Towage & Salvage, of Terneuzen, as part of that company's fleet expansion and she was renamed **Multratug 6**.

(Bernard McCall)

71

Of constant interest to tug enthusiasts on Southampton Water has been the US Army base at Hythe. This has seen many Army tugs brought across the Atlantic for refurbishment or reserve. In September 1993, the **Anzio** (LT 2085) was amongst the vessels at the base. The history of this tug has been difficult to trace but it seems to have been one of a group of thirteen similar tugs built by the National Steel and Shipbuilding Company (NASSCO) in San Diego, probably in 1955. They were based on a design popular during World War 2. The LT prefix denotes the class Large Tug. She has a Cooper-Bessemer engine of 1200bhp. What is known is that the **Anzio** was one of several members of the class to have been used in the mid-1960s as part of Project SHAD. This Project involved tests intended to show the vulnerability of ships to chemical and biological warfare agents. The tugs, apparently manned by navy rather than army personnel at the time, were involved in tests of tularamia, anthrax, parrot fever, Q fever, botulism and Rocky Mountain spotted fever. A deadly cocktail! By learning how these toxins would disperse, the military planners could improve procedures to protect crews and decontaminate ships. An American website suggests that she was refitted in 1996 and returned to service.

(Bernard McCall)

It was something of a surprise in the mid-1980s when Alexandra Towing purchased two identical secondhand tugs from Germany. The second of these was the 1976-built **Cornelie Wessels** from Emden which had spent the first two years of her life working for Petersen & Alpers in Hamburg as **Johanna**. Built by Mützelfeldwerft in Cuxhaven, she is powered by two Deutz engines giving a total of 2320bhp which drive two Schottel azimuthing propellers and provide a bollard pull of 36 tonnes. After purchase by Alexandra, she was renamed **Flying Osprey** and she is seen here thus named but in Adsteam colours assisting the container ship **MOL Promise** at Southampton's Container Terminal on 5 April 2003.

(Dominic McCall)

The **Teign C** is a very handy tug/workboat based, as her name suggests, in the attractive South Devon port of Teignmouth. Another Damen standard tug, she is of a class designated Stan Tug 1405. In addition to usual workboat duties, she is used for plough dredging and bed levelling. She also assists larger vessels using the port, the approach to which involves delicate navigation over a sand bar followed by a 120° turn at the mouth of the River Teign. A heavy pushbow can be used to ease ships alongside the quay if necessary. Her twin Cummins main engines provide 600bhp and she has a bollard pull of 8 tonnes, quite sufficient for the work she is required to do. She was photographed on 25 March 2002 as she approached the mouth of the Teign on her way out to meet the inbound Russian vessel **Pindushi**.

(Dominic McCall)

There can be few ship photographers who have failed to marvel at the splendid views to be had in the Cornish port of Fowey, a port which has become renowned throughout the world for its export of china clay. Tug lovers have especially enjoyed the port environs for the Fowey Harbour Commissioners have tended to operate tugs which have been ousted from other ports following replacement by more modern vessels. The **Tregeagle**, photographed passing the Bodinnick ferry on 10 April 2001, is a typical example. Built by J Lewis & Sons Ltd, Aberdeen, in 1964, she began life on the Clyde as the **Flying Demon** but moved to the east coast of Scotland in 1984 for a two-year spell named **Forth**. She was purchased by Fowey Harbour Commissioners in 1986 and has given excellent service since then. Her British Polar diesel engine delivers 1000bhp and drives a controllable pitch propeller. A modest bollard pull of only 15 tonnes is sufficient for the shiphandling duties at Fowey.

(Bernard McCall)

The tug fleet in Falmouth has traditionally been one of great interest for it has comprised older vessels displaced from their original area by more modern tonnage. The 1960-built *St Mawes* is a case in point. Built, like so many vessels appearing in this book, at the Hessle yard of Richard Dunston, she began life on the Thames as *Ionia* in the fleet of William Watkins Ltd. She survived the mergers which have been outlined and eventually entered the fleet of Alexandra Towing. In 1973, her propulsion machinery was updated. She was fitted with a controllable pitch propeller, Towmaster nozzle and multiple rudder system. After these modifications, she had a bollard pull of 22 tonnes. Having been sold to Falmouth Towage Ltd, she left the Thames on 26 November 1987 to a noisy send-off from other tugs. She worked under her original name for some time and was not officially given her new name until 9 May 1988. Here she is seen assisting the ferry *European Endeavour* which had just emerged from drydock on 2 April 1997. Just visible also is the *St Piran* whose history appears on page 22. Sold out of the Falmouth fleet in mid-2001, the *St Mawes* had the misfortune to go aground off the South Devon coast later in the year and has had a succession of owners since then.

(Bernard McCall)

After many years of purchasing good quality tugs from UK owners, Falmouth Ship Towage searched more extensively when it sought to upgrade its fleet at the start of the new millennium. The search led them to the fleet of Ocean Srl, of Trieste, which was willing to sell two of its tugs but only after delivery of new tonnage. These were sister vessels originally named *Comet* and *Cyclop* which had been built for Hapag Lloyd by F Schichau at Bremerhaven in 1967. When sold to Italy, they were renamed *Komet* and *Kiklop*. They each have two Deutz main engines with a total power output of 1580bhp driving two Voith Schneider propulsion units. This system provides a bollard pull of 20 tonnes. Falmouth had to wait eighteen months before its new tugs could be delivered. After arrival on 24 May 2001, they retained their previous identity but later that year, the *Komet* was renamed *Ancorva* while the *Kiklop* became *Percuil*. There was some surprise that they did not have the traditional saint names long associated with Falmouth tugs but Ancorva is a local anchorage and Percuil is a local river - and the initial letters of A & P are fitting because Falmouth Ship Towage is a wholly-owned subsidiary company of the A & P ship repair group. Our photograph shows the *Percuil* emerging from drydock on 3 November 2003.

(T & K Atkinson)

As we approach the end of the book, we look at two tugs whose primary role is not shiphandling in port approaches. The Holyhead Towing Company was established in 1962 as a yacht chandlery and has since grown into a much larger company offering a wide variety of maritime services. These include a small fleet of tugs used to support various civil engineering projects. No doubt the **Afon Braint** would have been working on such a project when photographed in the unusual setting of Hull Marina on 29 December 2003. The tug was built by Damen Shipyards in 1999 as **Knight Buster** and is another of the company's standard designs, being designated a "Shoalbuster 1907" type. She entered the Holyhead fleet in June 2002. She is driven by two Caterpillar engines with a total of 940bhp which drive two fixed-pitch propellers located in nozzles. This machinery gives her a bollard pull of 12.5 tonnes.

(Roy Cressey)

High-profile maritime casualties in the 1980s and 1990s led to calls for powerful tugs to be located in some key parts of the UK and to be on standby at all times in order to deal with any vessels in difficulties. The Maritime & Coastguard Agency has chartered several tugs for such a purpose since then. In 2001, Klyne Tugs, of Lowestoft, won an 8-year contract to provide four such emergency towing vessels (ETVs) to the Agency. One of these, the **Anglian Prince**, was well away from her usual sphere of operation when photographed in current Coastguard livery at Hull on 2 December 2002. Normally she is to be found in the area of Stornoway and the Minches. She was built at the Chung Wah shipyard, Hong Kong, and delivered to United Towing as **Salvageman** early in 1981. In April 1982, she was requisitioned by the UK Government for service during the Falklands campaign. There she served with distinction, and did not return to the UK until June 1984. In December 1989, she was sold to owners in Gibraltar but remained under United Towing management. In 1991, she was renamed **Hispania** and five years later entered the Klyne fleet as **Anglian Prince**. Powered by four Ruston diesels driving twin screws, she has a massive 170 tonne bollard pull which is essential for the kind of duties which she may be called up to perform.

(Roy Cressey)

The 1970s and 1980s saw the demise of many of the lighterage companies whose tugs and barges had been a familiar sight on the Thames for many years. It was in October 1984 that the Lee and Brentford Lighterage Co Ltd ceased to trade, its sole tug at the time being the **Revenge**. The company sought to offer a link between London's dock system and Brentford, from where the canal system could be accessed. This would reduce the pressure on London's congested roads. Such a plan deserved better. The **Revenge** was later sold to General Marine Ltd. She had joined the Lee and Brentford company in 1982 and had previously been part of the substantial Thames fleet of Wm Cory Lighterage Ltd. She was built in 1948. Her 330bhp engine provides a bollard pull of 6 tonnes. This characteristic Thames image, dating from October 2003, seems to be a suitable one with which to end the book.

(Bernard McCall)